Spot

Jack's cat

Spot

Jack's cat

3

Spot likes the cat.

Spot likes Jack's cat.

Up went the cat.
Up went Jack's cat.

Up went Spot.
Up, up, up he went.

Down went the cat.

Down went Jack's cat.

Down went Spot.

Down, down, down he went!

In went the cat.
In went Jack's cat.

In went Spot.
In he went.

Jack's cat helps Spot.

Spot likes Jack's cat, and

Jack's cat likes Spot!

12